VALERI SEPP

TALLINN

THE CITY OF LEGEND AND TRADITION

FELISTELLA

When embarking on a discovery tour of Estonia, the obvious place to start is Tallinn. Right next to the towering glass giants of high-rise hotels nestle small, cosy guest-houses, office blocks, brightly lit shop windows and quaint little restaurants offering the passing tourist a rich sampling of native cuisine. Small wooden houses in Tallinn coexist peacefully with knight's castles and modern architecture. Given the city's contrasts and variety, it's important to consider it from various perspectives and allow for time to feel and discover it, in all its detail. Tallinn is one of only a very few European cities still surrounded by a genuine fortress wall and well-preserved town gates.

The Estonian name of *Tallinn* is thought to have come from either the words *Taani Linn* ("Danish Town") or *Tali Linn* ("Winter Town") or even *Talu Linn* ("House, Farmstead-castle").

Prior to 1918, the town was known as *Reval*. Upon restoration of Estonia's independence it was renamed as Tallinn. The German and Swedish name *Re-*

val came from the neighbouring Estonian village named Ravala (*Rävala*, 13ᵗʰ century). Until that time, Tallinn had been historically referred to as *Lindanise* (Old Slavic), *Kesoniemi* (Finnish), and *Quoluwany* (Old Russian). It was the Arabic geographer and explorer, Al Idrisi, who first made mention of Tallinn, in 1154. In his travel notes entitled "Entertainment of One Yearning for Distant Travel" a description is given of a certain locality named *Quoluwany*.

Tallinn is situated on the shores of the Baltic Sea, just a few hours by air from the major European cities. With its delightful mix of wrought-iron signs, ornate weather vanes, curious hooks on walls (the purpose of which remains shrouded in history) and crooked window frames of ancient houses, it is clearly worthy of more than just a cursory glance. On the contrary, it demands a careful investigation and examination under the microscope.

The medieval city of Tallinn consists of two different cities, both

of which form a historical unit: **the Upper Town** (Toompea) and **the Lower Town**. Though closely linked with each other, both cities retained their own sets of laws. What was allowed to the residents of Toompea was forbidden to the merchants of the Lower Town and vice versa. Toompea was an independent and entirely isolated entity. It was the place of residence of the government ranks, military detachment, bishop and other clergy members. Among others who frequented Toompea were various vassals of the landlords who derived income from the manors and had numerous servants. The Lower Town was, in its turn, the place where wealthy merchants, prosperous (and less prosperous) artisans, as well as free citizens lived.

Three hundred years ago, "**Long Leg**" (*Pikk jalg*) street was the only path from one part of the city to the other, a passage both awkward and very narrow. "Long Leg" street did not have a stone wall, and, ice-covered in winter and full of slush in autumn, it was often quite dangerous. Clearly, the residents of Upper

⇩ *Upper Town (Toompea)*

Lower Town ⇨

⇧ *"Long Leg" street*

Linda ⇨

and Lower Towns were not particularly enthusiastic in visiting each other's homes.

Estonian peasants were serfs and belonged to their landlords. If a landlord was harsh and cruel, the peasants often fled to the Lower Town. If the peasant managed to hide from the landlord for one year and one day, according to city law he became a free person under the protection of the city.

According to legend, Tallinn was founded on a burial mound. This hill is called "Toompea" and is considered to be the burial site of Kalev, a legendary warrior-giant in Estonian mythology. Over the course of many months, his grieving widow, **Linda**, brought huge boulders to this burial place and in this way, Toompea hill was formed. Linda, tired from such enormous effort, sat down to rest and, herself, turned to stone. In 1920, on this site in Lindamagi park (*Lindamägi* — Linda Hill), the people of Tallinn erected a monument in memory of weeping Linda, created in 1880 by the Estonian sculptor A. Veytsenberg.

⇧ *Toompea Castle*

The park is surrounded by century-old linden trees and Linda's monument is decorated with an inscription in old Estonian language, dedicated to her unending grief and sorrow.

The construction of castles in Estonia began around the 13th century. Until that time, the only fortifications that existed were walled settlements. Invasion of Estonian land by the Germans and Danes changed the development of architecture abruptly and the first buildings in the Romanesque style appeared. As time went on, each self-respecting landowner built a castle for himself.

Since then, many towns and castles have been built and subsequently destroyed. However, many of them have survived to this day in the Estonian cities of Narva, Parnu and Rakvere and of course Tallinn is home to one of the most majestic castles of all: **Toompea Castle** (*Toompea loss*). Toompea hill was an ideal place for the construction of a fortress, and it was from the hill itself, that the structure got its name. The castle was built in the 13th – 14th centuries, and became a symbol of local authority, an authority that changed hands repeatedly on Toompea.

During this time, Upper Town was subjugated to the Danish kings. The Order of the Sword once again become part of the Danish state, after which it then became a part of the Livonian military religious orders for more than two hundred years. During the Livonian War, on the 27th of January, 1561, Polish forces occupied Toompea and it was placed under the control of the King of Poland for several months. On the 6th of June, 1561, Toompea and the Lower Town swore allegiance to the Swedish king, Eric XIV. Finally, on the 29th of September, 1710, the cities of both Upper and Lower Reval were invaded by Peter the First's troops and Estonia became part of Rus-

⇧ *"Pilsticker" (Spear Grinder)*

⇩ *Estonian Parliament*

sia for more than 200 years. Everyone who was a master of Toompea castle rebuilt it according to his own needs and tastes. The Livonian Military Religious Order (to which all knights were consecrated) combined the monastery and the fortress and created a castle. This structure had the usual monastery premises together with powerful fortifications, with four towers at each corner of the fortress. Their names are descriptive in their own right: "Landskrone" (The Crown of the State), "Pilsticker" (Spear Grinder), "Stür den Kerl" (Rout the Enemy) and "Pikk Hermann" (Tall Herman).

The tallest tower of the castle, **Tall Herman** (*Pikk Hermann*), is 45.6 meters high. There are 10 floors in the tower. The lower floors housed barns, the middle floors heated accommodations, the upper floors were designed for shooting from and storage of supplies, and at the very top was an open platform. The tower's name is derived from the German word "Lange Hermann" — Tall soldier or commander.

As time went on and the town grew richer, the danger of hostile attack also grew. From

⇧ *Long Leg gate tower*

1310 – 1355 a town wall was erected (which still survives today) and the moats surrounding the town were filled with water from Lake Ulemiste (*Ülemiste*). The wall was 6.5 metres high and about 2.3 metres thick and contained a system of interior defensive trenches. At the end of the 14th century, it was the general practice to build semicircular towers and quadrangular turrets on top of gates. Only one of these, the **Long Leg gate tower** (*Pika jala väravatorn*), built in 1380, has

⇦ *Governor's Garden (Kuberneri Aed)*

⇧ Tall Herman

survived. In the 15th century, they began to erect circular towers. The Tall Hermann tower is one example of this design. At present, the blue-black-and-white Estonian national flag is raised daily at dawn. However, it is raised no earlier than 7 a.m. and lowered no later than 10 p.m. The raising of the flag is performed to the music of the national hymn: "Mu isamaa, mu õnn ja room" ("My Fatherland — my happiness and joy"), and the lowering, to the song of "Mu isamaa armas" ("My beloved Fatherland").

⇩ "Short Leg" street

14

In 1454–1455 a wall was built along "Long Leg" street. The wooden gate tower of "**Short Leg**" (*Lühike jalg*) street was replaced by a quadrangular one of stone and Long Leg tower was also renovated. Both towers have survived until today and **Short Leg gate tower** (*Lühikese jala väravatorn*) has even retained its heavy oak door, covered with a multitude of hammered rivets, their broad heads facing towards Upper Town. There was a time when the tower had two such doors and a wrought iron grill, which was lowered by the guards at night. Because of this, the town wall that runs along Long Leg Street was called "Distrust Wall" by the townsfolk.

Initially, the oak door had been meant purely as a functional thing: it was closed each night and it drew a line between Toompea (Upper Town) and Lower Town. The door closes even today, though just once a year on the morning of the 15th of May, and for an entirely different purpose. From "above" (i.e. Upper Town) the Prime Minister knocks

⇩ *Old Town Days*

at the riveted door. From the opposite side (i.e. Lower Town) he hears a response from the Mayor, and the gate sweeps open. Such is the opening ceremony, with which celebrations begin on Tallinn's Day. Tallinn marks this day on the 15th of May. It was precisely on the 15th of May 1248, that Lubeck Town Law came into force, essentially granting Tallinn the right to self-government. Neither the Danish King nor the Order's magistrate were allowed to intervene in decisions taken by the Tallinn magistrate. Lubeck Law brought international standing to Tallinn. Until recently, Tallinn did not have its own holiday and the day was officially observed for the first time in 2002. Many interesting events take place on that day in the streets of the Old Town. The Town Hall Square becomes the focus of attention, where a diverse concert programme is carried out all day long. At the end of the month, the traditional Old Town Days are held.

The Old Town has been, and remains, the heart of Tallinn. It is fairly well preserved and therefore has been registered as an object of world heritage by UNESCO. The old medieval town

amazes visitors with its fairytale beauty and the labyrinth of narrow, crooked streets remains indelibly printed on the memory of all who come to the town.

In medieval times, the centre of the Old Town — **Town Hall Square** (*Raekoja plats*) — was always a busy market place. The moderately sized square is surrounded by a ring of ancient houses that have witnessed many events, from merry carnival festivities to cruel court proceedings. It was here, that news, laws and edicts were proclaimed. In old times, in the centre of the

⇧ *Town Hall*

⇩ *Town Hall Square*

square stood a pillory, where the hangman brought thieves, horse rustlers and criminals who had been sentenced to death. Today, the Town Hall Square is one of the liveliest spots in Tallinn. The main **Town Hall** (*Raekoda*), first mentioned in 1322, almost certainly used to stand exactly in its present-day location. Its present-day look was achieved after thorough reconstruction in 1402–1404, and in 2004, it marked its 600th anniversary.

The interior décor of the Town Hall, like its external architectural character, is simple. On

⇐⇓ *Burghers' Hall*

the ground floor there is a **Trade Hall,** in which merchants arranged their deals. The interior has changed slightly; however, there are still large chests along the walls and a huge map of trade routes on the wall, just as there were, years ago.

On the principal floor is the **Burghers' Hall.** During the Middle Ages, feasts were held here and city laws were read out. The hall doors were manufactured at the Tallinn grand piano factory, and so, are black, varnished and resemble a grand-piano lid. Some years ago, this hall was restored

Magistrate's Hall ⇨

⇧ *The interior décor of the Town Hall and dragon-head-shaped water spout*

and old paintings were exhibited. The hall was quite colourful in its day. The bright pattern on the columns has been restored, but actually the whole hall used to be very bright, the walls of the hall decorated with scenes of King Solomon's life. Nowadays, receptions and concerts are held here. **The Magistrate's Hall** is the most interesting hall of all. The city council used to gather here and this is the place where regulations and laws were passed. It is in this hall, particularly, that one can view some of the oldest furniture preserved in Tallinn, including valuable, artistically carved wooden benches. One 15th century bench has been preserved, decorated with a delicate openwork carving, with a frieze above it, with five medallions depicting the Prophets.

An example of some of the earliest Estonian carving can be seen on the side of the Ratmans' (members of the Magistrate) bench. Dating from the 14th century, it depicts the scene of Delilah, cutting Sampson's hair.

It was in the Town Hall that the

magistrate held its sittings and down through the ages, it was here, that some of the most important decisions affecting town life were made. Today, festive receptions and concerts take place in these premises. Notably, each month, the mayor welcomes young citizens and presents their birth certificates.

The most famous feature of the Tallinn Town Hall is its weather vane: "**Old Thomas**" (*Vana Toomas*), one of the symbols of Estonia's capital. Legend has it

"Old Thomas" ⇨
Great Sea Gate ⇩

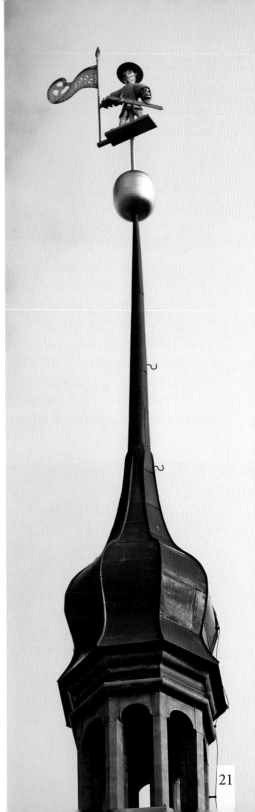

that each spring, on the square by the Great Sea Gate, an archery competition was held. The best marksman was awarded a large silver cup. Once, when venerable knights had lined up, had drawn their bows and were ready to shoot, the target suddenly fell, struck by someone else's arrow. As it turned out, the unknown archer was an ordinary youth from Tallinn, a local fellow by the name of Toomas. The mischievous youth was duly admonished and was forced to place the target back in its place. Surprisingly, the youth was not punished, however. Instead, he was offered a place in the town's guard, which, in those days, was a great honour for a poor man. Later, during the Livonian War, Toomas displayed heroism more than once, and earned his people's trust. In old age, he grew a prominent moustache and eventually took on the form of the gallant warrior on top of the Town Hall. Ever since then, the weather vane above the Town Hall has been called "Old Thomas". Tallinn's Town Hall, which gave the square its name, is the only Gothic town hall of its kind to have survived in the Baltics to the present day.

The Town Hall Pharmacy (*Raekoja apteek*) is one of the longest continually operating pharma-

cies in Europe. The chemist at the corner of the Town Hall Square was first mentioned in the chronicles of 1422. Through the ages, the exterior of this honourable building has not changed much and even today, from its walls come the fragrance and charm of centuries-old history. If you do visit the pharmacy, don't expect to be treated to some obscure bat and snake-skin mixture, but rather, to a glass of claret drawn from special spices, which was quite popular in the Middle Ages. The art of preparing healing remedies at the Town Hall Pharmacy has not been lost!

In ancient times, Tallinn was not

Town Hall Pharmacy ⇩

at all large. It grew slowly and ships rarely visited the port of Tallinn. This caused some distress to the people of Tallinn. They had dreams of developing into a large trade harbour and so, kept thinking of ways to bring attention to their town. One day it dawned on somebody to build a large church, with a bell tower higher than the world had ever seen. Ships would not fail to notice it from out on the open sea and would gladly visit Tallinn with their cargos of goods. The town's people received the idea enthusiastically. However, the matter remained, of finding a master prepared to undertake a job of such immense complexity. Then, suddenly, a tall stranger arrived on the scene, who promised to build such a church. This was all very well; however, the stranger seemed to be overcharging. He wanted so much gold as was hardly to be found in the whole of Tallinn. Then the strange master suggested the following: he would charge nothing, if they could discover his name. The townspeople promised to pay the amount, but, of course, they hoped to find out his name. Soon, the master set about his job. As he laid stones, the wall began to

St. Olav's Church ⇨

rise and soon an arch appeared. People tried to make friends with him, so as to learn his name, but he remained closed and unsociable. Meanwhile, the construction was reaching its end. The townspeople's fear grew. No one had yet been able to find out the builder's name and where should they find the necessary gold? There was nothing for it. They sent out a spy to visit his wife, in the hope of learning something. At first the spy was unsuccessful. However, one day, when going past the builder's wife's house, he heard her lulling her baby to sleep:

Sleep, my baby, sleep,
Soon Olev will be back home,
with his bag full of gold.

The spy hurried back to Tallinn with happy news: the builder's name was Olev! Just at that moment, the builder was at the top of the tower, attaching the cross to the ball. The town's people started calling him from the ground: "Olev! Olev! Do try harder! The cross is leaning! Fix it properly!" The builder was stunned. The townspeople had found out his

⇦⇩ *Interior of St. Olav's Church*

name, and his hopes of receiving his pay in gold were dashed! Horror-stricken, Olev unclasped his hands, let go of the cross and, losing his balance, fell headlong to the ground. As soon as he struck the ground, his body turned to stone and a toad and snake emerged from his mouth. They can both still be seen today, turned to stone, by the church wall. The church, however, came to be called "Oleviste," after the master who built it.

The first mention of the church dates back to 1267. Historians agree that it stood in its current location, the merchants' court, even in the 12th century. **St. Olav's Church** (*Oleviste kirik*) owes its name to the Norwegian King Olav Haraldson. Also, St. Olav was regarded as the patron and protector of seafarers. By the 16th century the height of St. Olav's was 159 metres (its steeple today rises to 124 m), which made it the highest structure in

the world at that time in history. The Church's steeple, soaring into the sky, could be seen from afar and served as an excellent navigational aid for seafarers. However, this lofty structure was also fraught with serious hazard. Eight times, throughout history, the church has been hit by lightning and three times, during a thunder storm, it was enveloped in flames. According to reports passed down through the generations, the glow of the fire was visible even from the shores of Finland.

The well-known chronicler, Balthasar Russow, recorded one other interesting fact, associated with the Church's history. In 1547, a group of tightrope walkers came to Tallinn. They stretched a very long rope between St. Olav's tower and the town wall and to the great amazement of the townspeople they began to perform

various acrobatic feats. In summer time, one can take the spiral staircase to the giddy heights of the observation platform on top of the church tower and enjoy the sights of old Tallinn.

From almost all points in the city one can see the soaring cupolas of the Orthodox **Cathedral of St. Alexander Nevsky** (*Püha Aleksander Nevski katedraal*), the largest church building in the Baltics. This beautiful, five-headed, three-altar temple, built to receive 1500 parishioners at a time, was designed in 1900 by

⇦⇩ *Interior of Cathedral of St. Alexander Nevsky*

the noted Russian architect Mihail Preobrazhensky. It was decided to dedicate the cathedral to St. Alexander Nevsky in honour of the miraculous salvation of the Czar, Alexander III and his family, in a horrible train crash on the 17th October, 1888.

The icons for the church were painted in the studio of Academician Alexander Novoskoltsev. In accordance with his sketches, St. Petersburg master, Emil Shteynke, made stained glass windows with images of the Saviour, Mother of God and John

⇦⇩ *Interior of Cathedral of St. Alexander Nevsky*

the Baptist, which were set in the windows of the main altar chapel. The façades of the cathedral are decorated with large mosaic icons, created by architect-academician A. N. Frolov. Two gilt bronze chandeliers in the aisles also decorate the cathedral. They are modelled after the famous chandelier in the Church of Our Saviour on the Bor, in the Moscow Kremlin. Murals were made by Grigory Prokofiev, the painter. The artist used glue, wax and oil paints, as well as pure gold plate. Two marble memorial plaques

were installed in the walls on both sides of the main entrance. The first one is to the construction of the Cathedral and the other is in honour of its consecration. Later, plaques were put in place in the memory of soldiers and sailors killed in various battles. To this

Interior of Cathedral of St. Alexander Nevsky ⇨ ⇩

day, the Cathedral has survived beautifully and is considered the most majestic of Orthodox monuments in Tallinn.

Just a short distance from Alexander Nevsky Cathedral is a shady, little square in the shadow of the town wall — the **Danish King's Garden** (*Taani Kuninga Aed*). It is perhaps interesting that each summer the Day of the Danish flag is celebrated here. This has to do with the legend that it was in Tallinn, on the 15th of July, 1219, that the Danes received their national flag, in the midst of battle. The campaign was not progressing well for the Danish forces. They were on the verge of defeat when suddenly, a red flag with a white cross descended upon them from the heavens. Of course, such divine support gave the Danes new strength and they went on to win the battle. It is noteworthy that this flag has become both the official flag of Denmark as well as the coat of arms of the city of Tallinn.

There are two distinct towers in the Danish King's Garden. At

Danish King's Garden ⇨

⇧ *Stables Tower*

⇧ *Maiden's Tower*

various times, one of them was called both the Stables and the Junker's tower. Nowadays, this tower bears the name of **Stables Tower** (*Tallitorn*). In the 17th century, its various levels were used as prison cells. The beautifully named **Maiden's Tower** (*Neitsitorn*) is also nearby. The tower was built in the second half of the 14th century, and has been repeatedly destroyed and rebuilt. In spite of its evocative name, the tower really didn't come to be referred to as the Maiden's Tower because of any romantic, medieval history. Its story, on the contrary, is rather more prosaic, for at one time, the tower was a prison for young ladies of easy virtue. Only about ten years ago, it was turned into a very popular café. However, most importantly, in the Maiden's Tower dwells a genuine, real live ghost! It has repeatedly been seen by the staff of the café and by late evening visitors. The ghost always appears at the same time at midnight. It flies from hall to hall, sighing heavily and moving furniture for some reason. Of course, everyone must decide for himself, whether they believe in ghosts or not!

Kiek in de Kök tower ⇧⇨

Not far from the Maiden's Tower is the **Kiek in de Kök** tower, a 15th century, Northern European design tower, which was once the most powerful gun turret on the entire coast of the Baltic Sea. The tower was mentioned for the first time in 1475 as "a new tower at the Haryu gate, opposite the horse watering trough." There was a time when the tower had considerable firepower: it had 24 battlements for heavy guns and 30 for handguns. It was a tower of mixed design: a defence structure for maintaining vertical fire, as was common in the pre-firearm era, as well as a structure with turrets, which were gradually coming into vogue. The tower played a very important role during the Livonian War, when the city was shelled by Ivan the Terrible's troops. If one stands facing the entrance, one can still see cannon balls, embedded in the walls. When the siege was over, several cannon balls from the Russian guns were mounted in the thick walls and remind us of those events to this day.

The history of the name of the tower is rather curious. Kiek in de Kök may be translated as "Look into the kitchen." When the traders brought the first coffee beans to Tallinn, the authorities allowed only those of high social standing to drink the new, rather expensive beverage. Supposedly, soldiers could look into any kitchen of the city from the top floor of the tower and special guards with telescopes were posted on top of Kiek in de Kök to keep watch in the mornings, to check whether simple townspeople, merchants and artisans brewed illicit coffee or not. Those who dared to break the law were severely punished. Today, the

⇩ *Fat Margaret tower*

tower houses a historical exhibit. While Kiek in de Kök was erected in compliance with the principles of vertical defence, the cannon tower **Fat Margaret** (*Paks Margareeta*) was built in 1510 – 1529 according to the principles of horizontal defence. With a diameter of 24 metres, the short, circular Fat Margaret tower was designed by the Westphalian master, Gert Koningk. Later, the tower was used as a storehouse, barracks, and from the late 18th century until 1917, it served as a prison. At present, the tower houses the Maritime Museum.

Great Sea Gate ⇨

Tallinn has always been, and remains, one of the oldest and best-preserved medieval cities in Europe. It embodies within itself the perfect blend of medieval churches, Gothic style houses and modern infrastructure.

Tallinn's town wall (*Tallinna linnamüür*) built in the 16th century is one of the most powerful defence fortifications in Northern Europe. It is 2350 metres long and has 45 towers in all, along its perimeter, including the front gate towers. Of the entire fortification system, 26 towers have survived to date, as well as 1,850 metres of the wall. The remainder has been destroyed by time and man.

The Viru Gates (*Viru väravad*) were built in the 14th century and have only partly survived. They are situated in the eastern part of the Town Wall that surrounds Tallinn's Old Town. These two towers, clothed in green, are

⇩ *Viru Gates*

⇩ *Tallinn's town wall*

"gates in time". They lead from a modern city, full of skyscrapers, to the historic and most fascinating part of Tallinn. Viru Street, with its numerous shops, cafés and restaurants, runs along the approximately 200 meters leading up to the Viru Gates.

Not far from the Alexander Nevsky Cathedral, stands the snow-white **Dome Cathedral** (*Toomkirik*), situated at **Cathedral Square** (*Kiriku plats*). This

is one of the oldest churches in Tallinn. According to historians, the original church on the site was a wooden structure, built by the Danes in 1219. Later, the Dominican monks arrived in Tallinn to start building a stone church. Soon after, during a clash between the Knights and supporters of the governor of the Pope, the monks were killed and construction was halted. In 1233 a letter was sent to Rome with a request to allow the construction of the temple to resume. This letter has survived and is the oldest written refer- ence source pertaining to the church. The importance of this church is underlined by the fact that under a 14th century decree, the fines imposed on parents who refused to send their children to school were used for the construction of three major urban sites: the castle, the Town Wall and the Dome cathedral. Originally, the cathedral belonged to the Roman Catholic Church, but became a Lutheran cathedral in 1561. The floorings of the Dome cathedral, which served as a burialvault for many centuries, are covered with old tombstones. Its

⇦⇩ *Dome Cathedral*

walls are hung with the emblems and coats of arms of families of nobility, whose members were buried here. Prominent members of the Guild of artisans had their burial places in Dome Cathedral as well, as evidenced by the plate depicting a bull figurine under the three heraldic lions of Tallinn (thus indicating that the buried persons belonged to a butcher shop).

By the entrance lies a tombstone with the inscription "Otto Yohann Tuve". Legend has it, that he was a hard drinker and wom-anizer. When dying, he ordered that he be buried by the entrance to the church, in the hopes that all who stepped on his tomb would pray for his sins. In return, he would beg God to carry out the wishes of the one treading his remains under foot.

It was German merchants, ar-

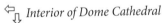
Interior of Dome Cathedral

riving in the city of Tallinn from Gotland Island, who founded **St. Nicholas' Church** (*Niguliste kirik*). The church acquired its original form in the 13th century and actually looked more like a fortress. The church was used as a warehouse for goods and was a place for settling trade deals. Throughout the medieval centuries, the church was richly decorated with numerous objects of art made in Lübeck, the capital of the Hanseatic League to which the city of Tallinn belonged. Historically, this was a Catholic church. However, during the period of the Reformation, it became a Lutheran church. St. Nicholas' Church is the only church in Lower Town fortunate enough to have survived the devastations of the Reformation period of 1523. Priceless exhibits of medieval age art are also on display in the church. The fragments of Bernt Notke's canvas "Dance of a Death" (end of the 15th century) are of great historical value. At the start of the Reformation, the theme of equality among noblemen and commoners was

⇓ *"Dance of a Death"*

widely propagated. This theme of equality among the representatives of the 24 estates existing at the time is also apparent in Notke's work. Death, in the form of a skeleton, is depicted alongside each character in the painting. The 30 meter long canvas, preserved in Lübeck, displays all 48 figures, whereas the Tallinn fragment comprises only 13 of those. However, this rare canvas is still of great value, since, of all other renditions of this work in the world, almost none have managed to survive.

St. Nicholas' Church ⇨

The Holy Spirit Church (*Püha Vaimu kirik*), situated near the Town Hall, is the smallest and oldest place of worship in Lower Town. It was first mentioned in 1316 and originally, was a refuge for the poor. The church's physical orientation was rather at odds with Christian traditions of the times. Usually, the churches were to be oriented with their axes pointing east-west. The Holy Spirit Church was erected, facing an entirely different direction: in a southwest to northeast orientation. The church was reconstructed and expanded many times and in the 17th century an octagonal spire was added. On the wall next to the entrance, Tallinn's oldest clock has been marking time for the past four centuries. It is the only street clock in the city — a most beautiful work of art, decorated with carvings and figures

⇩ *The Holy Spirit Church*

⇧ *The Paupers' Bible*

of the evangelists created by Christian Akkerman. One of the church's most valuable works of art is the altar, created in the year of 1483 by Lübeck master, Bernt Notke. In the centre of the altar is the sculptured composition, "The Descent of the Holy Spirit," and the side panels are decorated with paintings and sculptures of the saints. In the 17th century, pictorial decoration of the choir stalls was added, which included 57 pictures from the Biblical plot **"Biblia Pauperum"** (The Paupers' Bible). The Holy Spirit Church occupies a special place in the history of Estonia. The first sermons ever to be conducted in the Estonian language were delivered here, and the famous Estonian chronicler, Baltazar Russov, conducted worship services in the church. A catechism,

⇦ *Three Sisters Hotel*

published in 1535 by the church's pastor Johann Koell, is thought to be the first book published in the Estonian language.

House number 71 in Pikk Street was built in 1362 and witnessed plagues and fires, economic crises, wars and popular uprisings. Today, it is one of the most charming hotels in Tallinn, the **Three Sisters Hotel** (*Kolm õde*). Here a selection of exotic medieval elements has been kept intact: a wooden hoist once used for lifting bags with foodstuffs from outside to the upper storey has survived. Additionally, several old frescos were accidentally discovered on the ceiling, hidden beneath 14 coats of paints and wallpaper. Many celebrities have stayed at the Three Sisters Hotel, among them Britains's Queen Elizabeth II, during her visit to Tallinn in October 2006.

⇩ *Kadriorg Park*

Less than two kilometres from the centre of Tallinn are **Kadriorg** Park and Palace. Construction of the palace began on July 22, 1718 by order of the Russian Emperor, Peter the First, with the direct participation of the latter. The king himself laid down three bricks in the wall of the future palace (in the northeast corner of the building). They are still visible, due to the tradition of leaving them unplastered. The palace was built as a summer residence for the royal family and was named after the tsar's wife, Catherine the First, (*Kadriorg* means "Valley of Catherine" in Estonian). The Park was designed as a promenade for residents and visitors and consists of three parts. In the Upper garden are flower-beds and fountains. The Lower garden is located directly in front of the palace. Near the lower garden is the picturesque Swan Pond. Unfortunately, Peter the First did not live to see the completion of

⇩ *Kadriorg Palace*

the palace and after the death of the monarch the palace was only used on rare occasions. Russian emperors stayed here during visits to Tallinn. In 1919, after the overthrow of the tsarist regime, a museum was established in the palace. In 1991 a long period of restoration and repair began and on July 22, 2000, Kadriorg Art Museum opened within the palace, with exhibitions comprising more than 900 paintings of Russian and European pictorial art.